Food Rescue

Making Food Go Further

Written by Marilyn Woolley
with Marcus Godinho

Flying Start
to Literacy®

T0342929

Contents

Introduction

Many people do not have enough food to eat. But other people have so much food that they don't get to use it all and they throw some of it away. People can be very fussy about the food they buy and won't buy food that doesn't look perfect. This food is often thrown away, too.

A lot of food is thrown away every day.

Every day, an enormous amount of edible food is wasted. A lot of food that is thrown away is buried in landfills and this is bad for our environment.

What can be done about this problem? In what ways can we reduce waste? How can we make sure that this food gets to the people who need it?

Food waste and rubbish is buried at a landfill site.

Chapter 1

What a waste!

There are many ways that food is wasted.

People often buy too much food and then they cannot use all of it while it is fresh. When the food starts to get old, they throw it away.

Supermarkets only want to display food that looks perfect so they throw away any food that is getting too ripe or wilted, or not the right shape.

Food fact

In Australia, households throw away more than $5 billion worth of food each year. This includes more than $1 billion worth of fresh fruit and vegetables and about $870 million worth of meat and fish. More than $570 million worth of bread, pasta and rice is also thrown away, along with about $500 million worth of dairy products.

Some farmers throw away food they grow such as bananas or apples because they are too big, too small or an unusual shape, and supermarkets will not sell them. Most fruit and vegetables are sorted into grades from the highest to the lowest in terms of quality, shape and appearance. Only the best grades of fruit and vegetables are packed in boxes for people to buy. But the lower grades of fruit and vegetables are still edible and nutritious.

Some restaurants have food that is not used. This leftover food is thrown away.

Chapter 2

Saving food and helping people

What happens to food that cannot be sold? Some organisations collect food that farms, supermarkets, bakeries, markets and large food manufacturers cannot sell. They take it to big kitchens where volunteers make meals for people who don't have enough food

The meals are distributed to these people by charities that run food banks, soup vans, school breakfast programs or refuges.
Some of these organisations distribute food in a number of states or across a whole country; others work hard to feed people in just one city.

There are many food rescue organisations around the world. In some countries there are national programs that collect prepared and perishable food from food outlets and take it to charities.

Truck drivers in different places rescue millions of kilograms of fresh food and vegetables each year. Other people work in kitchens to cut up some of this food and make it into meals.

In the USA, workers at The San Francisco Food Bank collect 60 tonnes of leftover food from businesses each year. Most of this can be given to people in the San Francisco area who don't have enough food.

Chapter 3

Sharing and caring

In Melbourne, Australia, Marcus Godinho leads another food rescue organisation called FareShare. Marcus talks about how he and his volunteers collect leftover food from 100 businesses across the city, cook it and deliver it to where it is needed.

Marcus Godinho

Q: What sort of food do you collect and where does it come from?

A: FareShare has five vans with volunteer drivers who collect food from farms, supermarkets, markets, bakeries and other businesses. Some of this food may have a slight bruise or blemish or it may be close to its "use-by" date.

We receive eggs from a large egg farm. This farm gives us the eggs that they cannot sell because they are too big, too small or have double yolks.

We collect cans and packets of food because they are getting close to their "use-by" dates, the packaging has been damaged or the labels are incorrect.

Q: What sort of kitchen do you need to prepare all the food?

A: We have a big kitchen with lots of equipment. There are two very large ovens, a walk-in cool room and freezer, a lot of benches, knives, bowls, and a giant saucepan that can hold food for 200 people.

Q: Who are your kitchen volunteers and what do they do?

A: Our volunteers in the kitchen are mostly older people who have retired, students and those in their 20s and 30s who volunteer after work.

Food fact

In one year, over 3000 people volunteer with FareShare.

FareShare volunteers do these jobs:

- Cut vegetables and meat
- Roll out pastry
- Open tins
- Make mixes for pies and sausage rolls
- Load and unload the ovens
- Wash dishes and clean the kitchen
- Pack meals
- Drive vehicles to collect food and drop off meals to charities
- Help in the warehouse

Q: What sort of meals do the volunteers make?

A: Each day our volunteers cook 2000 meals such as casseroles, stir-fries, pies and quiches. The meals are filled with vegetables, high-fibr breadcrumbs, meat, cheese and eggs. Many people who need our meals don't have enougl protein and fibre in their diet, so we make meals that contain both of these things.

Q: Where are these meals taken?

A: 150 charities receive food from FareShare – we deliver it to some charities, and other charities collect it from us. Some charities hand out our meals as part of a food parcel for people to take home. Others serve the meals in large dining rooms. All of our meals are given away free of charge.

Food fact

FareShare distributes one million free meals to charities each year.

Q: How do you pay to transport the food and meals?

A: We rely on donations because we do not receive any funds from the government. Some people carry out fundraisers at school and work; and some companies and individuals donate money to us. There are restaurants that donate some of the money they make from each meal they sell.

Food fact

Each year an average of 370 000 people run out of food in the state of Victoria, Australia, and cannot afford their next meal.

Chapter 4

No more waste at home

There are many ways to make sure you don't waste food at home.

Buy what you need

Some families try to reduce waste by only buying the food that they really need. A good way to do this is to look in the fridge before shopping to check what you have and what needs to be used soon. Then make a shopping list and stick to it.

When putting away new food items, place them at the back of the refrigerator or pantry. This means older items get used first.

Food fact

In Australian households, one tenth of the food that is bought is wasted.

Making food go further

There are lots of ways to use food that is no longer fresh. You can make banana bread or smoothies with very ripe bananas. Stale bread can be made into breadcrumbs and frozen, to be used later in recipes. Older vegetables can be used to make soups, curries and stir-fries, which can then be frozen to eat another time.

When using a recipe, the cook can think about how many people will be eating the food, then make exactly the right amount, rather than following the portions in the recipe. If there are leftovers, they can be taken to school and work for lunch.

Recycle food scraps

Some people try to reduce food waste by recycling food scraps at home. They make compost by combining soil, earthworms and food scraps in a compost bin.

Earthworms like to eat things that were once alive and growing, such as vegetable and fruit scraps. They pass this food through their bodies into the soil.

As earthworms eat
the food scraps, they
dig tunnels. This
helps improve the
soil, as air and water
pass through these
tunnels. People can
then use this soil in
their gardens.

Conclusion

As the world's population grows, so does the number of people who don't have enough food. But in some countries, the amount of food that is wasted is also increasing.

Groups and organisations are taking action and thinking up new ways to collect food, and make meals for people who need them. Other people have set up large composting programs to get rid of food waste.

We can take action too. We can help the environment and save money by reducing the amount of food we throw away at home.

Glossary

compost a mixture of rotting leaves, fruit and vegetables, and animal droppings that is used to make soil healthier

donation money that is given for a good cause

landfill a place used to dump a large amount of rubbish

manufacturer a company or person who makes something

perishable able to go rotten in a short time

refuge a place where people who have had to leave their homes for their own safety can go for food and shelter

rescue to save something from danger or harm

volunteer people who work without being paid

A note from the author

To find some of the information in this book, Marcus and I looked at surveys from government agencies on the amount of food wasted in some countries. In Australia and the USA, households waste over one-tenth of the food they buy. An average family of four throws away $600 worth of meat, fruit, vegetables, cereal and flour or rice each year.

We discovered that many countries around the world have organisations that collect food that is not used and redistribute it to those who need it.

We also looked at the work of some groups to compost waste food, and research by various food charities into the types of assistance they provide to people.